The Black Masculinist:

It is a Movement

by Erika Prelow

Table of Content

Dedication	*3*
Epigraph: Daniel Patrick Moynihan	*4*
Blissful Gray	*5*
Preface	*6*
The Black Masculinist Movement	*9*
Race, Religion, and Politics	*18*
The Civil War: Black Men vs Black Women	*25*
Marriage Rates and Gender Dynamics	*30*
Religion, Family Separation, and the Complexities of Submission	*32*
Education and Family Dynamics	*40*
The Black Feminist Movement	*43*
Incentivized Welfare and the Black Family Structure	*46*
The Influence of Black Masculinist Social Media Platforms	*50*
Internal Community Dynamics	*54*
The Shifting Political Allegiances of Black Men	*61*
The Adultification of Black Children: Breaking the Cycle	*72*
The Interdependence of Black Masculinism and Black Feminism	*81*
The Evolution of Black Love: Redefining Need and Independence	*87*
Prologue	*91*
My Family: The Good Old Days	*96*
References	*99*

To my Moon and Sun, with Love.

There is one unmistakable lesson in American history; a community that allows a large number of young men to grow up in broken families, dominated by women, never acquiring any stable relationship to male authority, never acquiring any set of rational expectations about the future - that community asks for and gets chaos.
Daniel Patrick Moynihan

Blissful Gray

A formidable man I looked up too;

Engine stopped in the driveway,

The dancing stopped in the house,

We scattered like roaches into silos.

Rooms occupied by empty vessels,

Longing to be loved and validated,

Momma knew I wanted him to value me,

Unbeknownst then, momma craved the same.

We went silent to give him *his* space,

Space he filled with vast vexations,

Festering from childhood to now,

A grown man in need of repair.

Lashes from striking out…batter up,

Body flailing and momma squinching

Impression left an indelible mark,

To just hear the jiggling belt made me buckle

A formidable man I still look up too,

Living with the white noise of a black man,

Was not easy but we now live in a world of blissful gray.

PREFACE

When I was 16, I learned that my father had been drafted into the Vietnam War at 20. It struck me how close in age he was to me at that time. I couldn't imagine being sent to fight on the frontlines at that age, especially with little more than the inexperience of a young man from Natchitoches, Louisiana. Later, my father opened up about his time in combat—how he was wounded in battle, how he lost a dear friend, and how, when he finally came home, the country didn't offer him the welcome he deserved.

The more I thought about it, the more I wished I had done something to show him how much he mattered—something that truly honored his sacrifices. Decades later, I dreamed of throwing a "Welcome Home" parade not just for him, but for every black soldier who returned to a nation that failed to acknowledge their valor and patriotism. He came back carrying wounds, both visible and invisible, yet despite the trauma, he devoted himself to raising his children with unwavering love and care. He rarely spoke of his pain, but I saw it in the quiet moments, in the heaviness of his silence. Even so, he pressed on, determined to give us a life far better than the one he had known.

Through it all, I love his actual heart—the quiet, steadfast courage that defined him. I admire how he gave everything, not just in battle, but in life, in raising us. And I respect his Purple Heart, not just as a medal for his wounds, but as a symbol of the deep, unspoken sacrifice he made, one that went far beyond the battlefield.

I wish I had understood it all sooner—the depth of what he had gone through, the quiet strength he carried, the way he tried to shield us from his own darkness. In many ways, he was still that young man from Natchitoches, carrying the scars of war but doing his best to not allow them to define him. His sacrifice was profound, not just in battle, but in the way he chose to keep fighting for us every day.

I write this as his daughter, but also a sister to black brothers, a partner to a black man, a mother of a black son, and an aunt to black boys. Love and understanding drive my exploration of this topic, not malice or criticism. Society weaponizes black men's skin and vilifies their existence, portraying the black male body as a threat rather than celebrating its humanity.

While black feminism dominates podcasts, social media, and various platforms, "black-masculinism" remains largely absent from popular discourse. Even spellcheck marks it as an error, suggesting erasure or replacement. This publication aims to legitimize conversations about black masculinism and elevate this vital topic to its rightful place in mainstream discourse.

Black men face complex challenges shaped by numerous societal forces. Their behaviors and characteristics emerge from a rich tapestry of culture, history, and personal experiences. Understanding these dimensions helps us develop a more nuanced perspective that challenges stereotypes and acknowledges the diversity of black male experiences.

I encourage readers to join these conversations, recognizing that discussions about black masculinism matter not only for black men but for our entire community. Together, we can build understanding, foster connection, and promote healing, creating a more inclusive and empathetic society.

To name a thing is to give it power. Unknown

The Black Masculinist Movement

When my little brother was about eight years old, three girls from across the street, who had a crush on him, regularly ganged up on him and hit him. Although I was older and capable of stepping in, I knew it wouldn't have been fair to defend him by hitting the girls myself. One day, I heard a commotion outside and looked out the window. There he was, cornered by the girls, visibly frustrated. But this time, instead of enduring it, he hit one of them back.

The girls ran home, crying, and their mother came across the street to confront my brother and talk to my mom. although my brother had been taught never to hit girls, my mother, while acknowledging he was wrong, also pointed out, "they hit him so much every day."

This incident has stayed with me into adulthood, often returning as I reflect on the challenges black men face. How much punching down does the world have to do to black men before they push back? That day, my brother pushed back--and today, black men are doing the same. The weight of persistent attacks, whether physical, emotional, or systemic, eventually forces a response. It's not just retaliation; it's a refusal to remain cornered, a demand to be seen, heard, and respected.

While engaging with social media, I noticed a troubling contradiction: many black men, who expressed disdain for black feminists, exhibited similar behaviors and attitudes. Some of these men, however, were correct in their protests while other black men found common ground with black feminists in advocating for shared causes. The more I observed, the more a term began to resonate with me: black masculinist.

Black masculinists are primarily black men who center the unique challenges and experiences of black men in their advocacy. Their perspectives vary widely. Some are seen as empowering advocates for black men's rights, while others hold controversial, divisive views. Regardless, black masculinists come from diverse backgrounds and identities, supported by family, friends, and allies who share their mission to uplift black men in society.

Many black masculinists focus on dismantling systemic barriers that disproportionately affect black men, such as mass incarceration, economic inequality, and the stigma surrounding mental health. They aim to create opportunities for black men to thrive by fostering personal development, resilience, and community solidarity. For them, the movement serves as a tool for empowerment—helping black men reclaim agency over their lives and futures.

Others, however, adopt a more confrontational approach, critiquing mainstream social justice movements for failing to center black men's experiences. These men often argue that black men's struggles are sidelined in favor of issues more commonly associated with black women, leading to tension within broader social justice circles. This divide highlights the diversity of views within the black masculinist movement, with some advocating for a more inclusive approach that acknowledges both black men's and black women's struggles.

Historically, black men have been subjected to harmful stereotypes, particularly from European societies that used eugenics, pseudo-science, and racial superiority ideologies to justify slavery, segregation, and criminalization. These degrading portrayals—depicting black men as shiftless, violent, and absent fathers—were designed to uphold white supremacy and deny black men full citizenship and humanity. At the same time, black men have been fetishized for their perceived strength and physicality, further complicating society's contradictory relationship with them.

In response to these dehumanizing narratives, black men have consistently fought to reclaim their dignity and humanity. Unlike Black women, who have been able to find some degree of inclusion within mainstream feminist movements, black men often face a unique form of invisibility. Society tends to assume that black men benefit from the same masculine privileges as white men, yet the privileges of white masculinity rarely extend to them. While black men have long fought for recognition and equal rights, their struggles have not coalesced into a widely supported formal movement or framework.

This absence of a coherent black masculinist movement is rooted in the lack of societal structures that would support it. White men, positioned at the top of America's racial and gender hierarchies, have not faced the same degree of systemic oppression, and therefore have not developed a "masculine struggle" akin to that of black men. As a result, black men's efforts for justice remain isolated, their struggles largely invisible and misunderstood. This invisibility fosters deep frustration.

Social media has become a vital platform where many black men articulate their frustrations, pain, and anger. These platforms are critical for confronting the contradictions inherent in black masculinity. On one hand, society fetishizes black men, expecting them to embody hyper-masculinity—strength, aggression, and stoicism—while, on the other, it denies them the power and privileges typically associated with these traits. The gap between societal expectations and lived reality often results in significant emotional and psychological harm for many black men.

The black masculinist movement is not invisible because black men lack awareness of their oppression. On the contrary, black men have a deep understanding of their struggles, but without the language or space to express their needs and aspirations, their frustrations often intensify. Naming their struggle, acknowledging it for what it is, becomes an essential act of resistance. To give their collective struggle a name is to force society to recognize it, and demand action.

Black men are expected to navigate a world that devalues them, while also adhering to contradictory standards of masculinity. Society demands strength without vulnerability, protection without power, and invulnerability in the face of constant threat. These unacknowledged contradictions generate immense emotional strain, trapping black men in a cycle of damage—attempting to meet oppressive expectations without the opportunity for genuine healing.

The rising suicide rates among black men in recent years underscore the emotional toll of these contradictions. While the exact reasons are difficult to pinpoint, many black men do not leave behind notes, though their cries for help are evident. Several underlying factors contribute to this crisis, including the sense of being unseen, as their issues are often eclipsed by the focus on the struggles of black women. In addition, structural problems like mass incarceration and high unemployment further isolate black men, reinforcing their marginalization.

Many black men grow up in single-parent households, typically raised by mothers who face significant financial and social challenges. From a young age, they internalize the expectation that men must work and provide. Observing their mothers struggle without male financial support drives a sense of responsibility to help. For many, this pressure leads to illicit or precarious forms of income, like drug dealing or hustling, while those who find legal work often balance jobs with school, leading to disengagement and poorer academic outcomes. Studies show that this struggle heightens the risk of entering the school-to-prison pipeline, contributing to a cycle of systemic marginalization (Alexander, 2012).

This persistent economic strain fosters a cycle of "peripheral poverty," where black men remain stuck, barely getting by rather than achieving financial security or upward mobility. The resulting mental and emotional toll is immense. With limited access to mental health resources and support, many black men experience feelings of hopelessness, pushing some to contemplate suicide as an escape from an unrelenting battle. In a society that ignores their struggles, black men are growing weary of merely surviving.

This publication seeks to legitimize and amplify the black masculinist movement. It explores the unique challenges black men face as they navigate a world that exploits and fears them. Their struggles, though often overlooked, deserve the same recognition, advocacy, and justice afforded to other marginalized groups. By naming this movement, we begin to acknowledge black men as complex, fully human individuals worthy of dignity, empathy, and full citizenship.

Black men are expected to embody ideals of hyper-masculinity—strength, stoicism, aggression—yet are denied the privileges that typically accompany these traits in white men. Their oppression is both racial and gendered, creating an intersectional struggle that lacks a framework within existing social movements. While black women have been able to align with mainstream feminism, despite marginalization, black men have not found a comparable movement to address their unique intersectional struggles.

The emasculation of black men—from the historical separation of families to modern systemic oppression—remains central to their marginalization. Society demands they fulfill roles of strength and protection while simultaneously denying them the power to do so. This contradiction creates profound tension and emotional distress, shaping the black male experience of masculinity in America. To address this, we must first name the black masculinist struggle, recognizing it as a critical part of the broader fight for racial and gender justice.

Race, Religion, and Politics

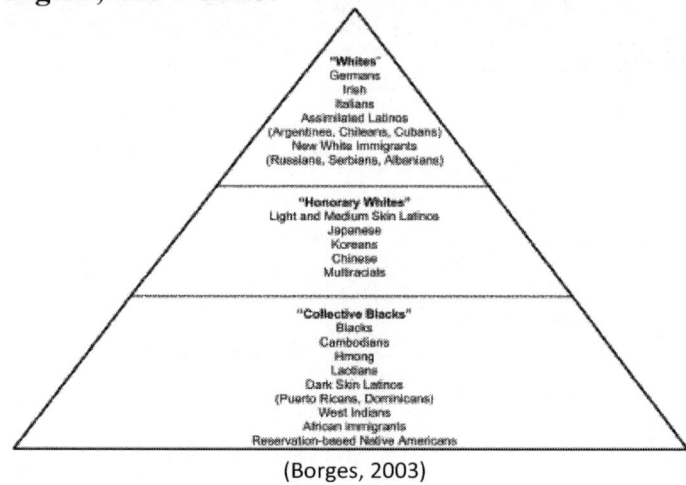

```
                    "Whites"
                    Germans
                     Irish
                    Italians
               Assimilated Latinos
          (Argentines, Chileans, Cubans)
              New White Immigrants
         (Russians, Serbians, Albanians)

                "Honorary Whites"
           Light and Medium Skin Latinos
                   Japanese
                   Koreans
                   Chinese
                  Multiracials

                "Collective Blacks"
                    Blacks
                  Cambodians
                    Hmong
                   Laotians
                Dark Skin Latinos
            (Puerto Ricans, Dominicans)
                  West Indians
                African Immigrants
          Reservation-based Native Americans
```
(Borges, 2003)

  Race, as a social construct, has been at the heart of many societal issues, driving division, inequality, and conflict. Historically, race was artificially created to categorize, control, and caste people, often with the goal of maintaining power structures that benefit a select few. By assigning value to skin color and creating rigid racial categories, societies established hierarchies that continue to shape economic, political, and social realities. These divisions breed prejudice, mistrust, and inequality, all of which hinder empathy and unity among people. Once something is divided by such measures, it may be possible to bring it back together, but the effort will be fraught with challenges. The resulting fractures and scars are often long-lasting, complicating the path to true reconciliation and unity.

Religion, while a profound source of identity, culture, and community, has also been used throughout history to justify power, control, and domination. Religious differences have been manipulated to create in-groups and out-groups, further driving wedges between communities. While faith can provide purpose and moral guidance, it has also served as a tool to justify wars, discrimination, and exclusion. The challenge of reconciliation across religious divides requires more than mere tolerance; it demands an active commitment to understanding and accepting one another's differences.

Politics, meant to organize society and protect citizens' rights, often intensifies these divisions rather than healing them. Political systems frequently exploit race and religion to gain control, spread divisive rhetoric, and serve narrow interests. Rather than uniting people for the common good, politics has often driven polarization, with communities separated by ideology rather than shared human needs. Instead of fostering cooperation and common purpose, political discourse too often fuels conflict and division.

The social construct of race continues to control and divide society with tremendous force, despite lacking any scientific basis. In America, the racial and gender hierarchy places white men at the apex, with white women occupying the next tier, while systematically positioning black men and women at the bottom. This structure, deeply entrenched in racism and misogyny, creates interlocking systems of oppression that perpetuate social inequities. These systemic barriers have far-reaching consequences, influencing access to education, healthcare, economic opportunities, and even personal safety.

The impact of these divisions infiltrates every aspect of American life. Discriminatory practices limit Black-Americans' access to quality education, high-paying jobs, and vital social resources. Banks deny mortgages to qualified black applicants at higher rates than white applicants with similar credentials. Employers overlook black candidates for promotions and leadership positions. Law enforcement disproportionately stops, searches, and uses force against black individuals. Healthcare providers often dismiss or minimize the symptoms and concerns of black patients, perpetuating health disparities.

These daily encounters with discrimination shape both the way society views Black-Americans and how Black-Americans view themselves. Media representations often reinforce harmful stereotypes, portraying black people as less capable, less professional, or more threatening than their white counterparts. Schools and workplaces frequently penalize black people for expressing themselves in ways that deviate from mainstream expectations, such as wearing natural hairstyles or speaking in African American Vernacular English (AAVE). These persistent societal messages can deeply affect self-image, career aspirations, and mental health within black communities, making it even more difficult to break free from the cycle of marginalization.

Black men, in particular, occupy a unique and precarious position within America's racial and gender hierarchy. Society views them as physical threats while simultaneously denying them the societal privileges that typically come with masculinity. White men enjoy authority, autonomy, and control, while black men face constant barriers to accessing these same privileges. Society demands that black men demonstrate strength, dominance, and resilience, yet systematically strips them of the power, respect, and opportunities typically associated with masculinity. This creates a profound paradox: Black men are expected to perform masculinity without the accompanying rights and freedoms.

This hierarchy often creates tension between black men and women, complicating their relationships and mutual support. While both black men and women face racial oppression, black women also contend with the added burden of gender-based discrimination. White women, while also oppressed by patriarchy, benefit from racial privilege, which complicates their pursuit of equality. Their struggle tends to focus on achieving parity with white men, often sidelining the broader intersectional struggles that black men and women face.

In contrast, black women navigate a dual struggle—facing both racial and gender oppression. Society expects them to champion both racial justice and women's rights, yet their specific challenges are often overlooked. In the process, black women are sometimes asked to downplay their own struggles to uplift black men, mirroring dynamics seen in white feminist movements. Historically, white women's alignment with white patriarchal structures has ensured that white men remain in power, preserving their own racial privilege.

However, it is essential to recognize that both black men and women face systemic barriers that can divide but also create opportunities for solidarity. By acknowledging and addressing the unique struggles of each group, we can foster a more inclusive and supportive environment that empowers both black men and women. This involves not only validating the experiences of black women but also providing space for black men to confront their own challenges without diminishing the voices or contributions of black women.

The path forward lies in building alliances that recognize and honor the strengths and resilience of both black men and women. We will never completely dismantle the hierarchical structures that divide us, but we must first acknowledge their existence and the historical reasons they were created. These structures were designed to perpetuate division and inequality, and understanding their origins is key to challenging their ongoing influence.

We cannot expect others, or any political party, to advocate for a more just and equitable society for all if we remain so deeply fractured. We cannot ask the world to "fix" us when it is the root of our divisions. To move forward, we must first value each other's humanity, recognizing that the constructs of race, gender, and power are deeply embedded in our histories, institutions, and beliefs. While erasing these constructs entirely may not be possible, acknowledging and confronting them is essential.

Through collective effort, we can begin to transcend prejudice and division. We must work to create a society that celebrates our shared humanity, rather than clinging to superficial differences. Only by understanding the structures that divide us and challenging their influence can we move toward the unity and justice we all deserve. This is not an easy task, but it is necessary if we are to build a future where everyone, regardless of race or gender, can live with dignity and freedom.

NEGRO WOMEN TO BE PUT TO WORK

City Ordinance Soon Be Passed Requiring Them to be Regularly Employed

MANY COMPLAINTS

Regardless of whether they want to or have to, able bodied negro women in Greenville who are not regularly employed are to be put to work, put in jail or fined heavily. At its special meeting yesterday afternoon City Council discussed the situation with regard to this class of loafers at some length, and it seemed that all members of Council were agreed that steps should be taken to compel them to engage in some useful occupation. It was decided that an ordinance, similar to the one now in force requiring all able-bodied men to work at least five days per week, should be passed with regard to these women. Such an ordinance will be prepared and voted on at the next regular meeting of Council.

A number of complaints have come to members of Council of negro women who are not at work and who refuse employment when it is offered them, the result being that it is exceedingly difficult for families who need cooks and laundresses to get them. Wives of colored soldiers, getting a monthly allowance from the Government, have a number of them, declined to work on the ground that they can get along without working, according to reports. Others have flatly refused jobs without giving any reason whatever, while still others pretend that they are employed when, as a matter of fact, they derive a living from illegitimate means.

The proposed ordinance will require them all to carry a labor identification card showing that they are regularly and usefully employed, and the labor inspectors and police will be charged with the duty of rigidly enforcing the law.

The Greenville News (1918) highlights the forced entry of Black women into the workforce during World War I, shedding light on their pivotal role in supporting the war effort and the broader societal shifts that followed.

The Civil War: Black Men vs Black Women

Modern black men often point to feminism as the source of division between black men and women, blaming black women for their involvement in the feminist movement. However, this narrative oversimplifies the roots of this divide within the black community. While the feminist movement certainly introduced new dynamics, it did not originate the fragmentation of black families. In fact, this unraveling began much earlier, as evidenced by a 1918 article in *The Greenville News*, which highlighted that black women were forced into the workforce during World War I (The Greenville News, 1918).

Both black and white women worked during World War II; however, white women were often able to secure less labor-intensive and cushioned positions compared to black women. The positions provided to white women upheld the notion of their femininity, while the roles taken on by black women reinforced stereotypes of them as impervious to pain and hard work, further defeminizing them (Williams, 2021). During this time, many black women preferred factory jobs over domestic work, seeking better pay and working conditions.

Deeper fractures occurred during the post-Civil War era, when systemic efforts to dismantle the black family structure began to take hold. During and after the Civil War (1861-1865), black men fought valiantly in America's wars, serving in regiments like the Buffalo Soldiers and the Harlem Hellfighters, often in pursuit of civil rights and recognition of their humanity and patriotism. Despite their sacrifices, the outcomes for black families starkly contrasted with those of their white counterparts. While white men returned to the family structures as they had left it; however, many black men found their wives coerced into the workforce, creating a new norm where black women assumed dual roles as both caretakers and breadwinners.

This shift was not merely a byproduct of war; it was a deliberate strategy aimed at further emasculating black men. By removing black men from their traditional roles as heads of households and promoting black women's financial

independence, systemic forces drove a wedge between black men and women. When these men returned from battle, they encountered significant barriers to employment. The G.I. Bill, enacted in 1944, often excluded black veterans due to systemic racism. While their white counterparts enjoyed job security and access to education, many black men struggled to provide for their families (U.S. Department of Veterans Affairs, n.d.).

The post-Civil War era laid bare the painful reality of economic inequality for black men. Despite their sacrifices, black veterans faced racial discrimination in the job market. A 2018 report from the Economic Policy Institute revealed that black men are more than twice as likely to be unemployed compared to white men, highlighting ongoing disparities (Economic Policy Institute, 2018). Employers frequently hesitated to hire black men, preferring to give jobs to their white counterparts, which further marginalized black men within their communities. With limited access to job opportunities—especially in the South—black men grappled with feelings of inadequacy and failure, unable to fulfill the traditional role of provider. In many ways, the success of black women in the workforce was a direct result of systemic forces designed to keep black men down.

This forced reliance on black women reshaped the dynamics of black families and relationships. As black women became the primary breadwinners, many black men felt increasingly emasculated. The cultural expectation for men to be protectors and providers was challenged, leaving them feeling stripped of their masculinity. This shift laid the groundwork for modern-day tensions between black men and women, who continue to navigate societal pressures to conform to traditional gender roles in an environment where such roles are often denied to them.

The implications of this history extend far beyond individual families; they permeate the collective consciousness of the black community. By understanding these dynamics, we can better address the ongoing struggles and conflicts stemming from this legacy, recognizing that the fight for equality and justice continues to affect both black men and women today. By acknowledging this shared history, we can foster greater unity and collaboration in the pursuit of a more equitable future for all.

Marriage Rates and Gender Dynamics

During the post-Civil War era, black men and women married at higher rates than their white counterparts. The desire for family unity after the abolition of slavery was strong. Freed black individuals sought to formalize their relationships and build communities, reflecting a deep commitment to family bonds. Despite these robust marriage rates, the economic conditions and systemic racism faced by black men undermined their ability to fulfill traditional family roles. This shift became more pronounced as black women increasingly took on roles outside the home, laying the groundwork for modern gender tensions.

In American history, fluctuations in marriage rates often mirrored economic conditions and cultural shifts. For instance, according to the U.S. Census Bureau, in 1890, approximately 58% of black adults were married compared to 47% of white adults (U.S. Census Bureau, 1890). During the Great Depression and World War II, marriage rates dipped for both black and white communities. However, even amid these economic challenges, black marriage rates remained relatively strong in some regions, bolstered by a deep-rooted desire for family and stability.

A 2020 report from the National Center for Family & Marriage Research revealed that black marriage rates were about 27% in 2018, compared to 48% for white individuals, reflecting ongoing disparities shaped by systemic factors (Lichter et al., 2020). Yet, even these strong unions could not escape the pressures of systemic oppression. Many black women had to work, often creating households where children—referred to as "latchkey kids"—were left to fend for themselves while parents toiled. According to the Annie E. Casey Foundation, in 2018, nearly 64% of black children lived in single-parent households, further straining the already fragile balance between gender roles within the black community (Annie E. Casey Foundation, 2019).

This complex interplay between marriage, economic hardship, and gender dynamics highlights the persistent challenges faced by black families. As black women assumed dual roles as breadwinners and caretakers, the traditional expectations of black men as providers and protectors were often disrupted, contributing to the modern tensions observed within the community.

Religion, Family Separation, and the Complexities of Submission

Religion has historically been used to reinforce societal inequalities, offering divine justification for maintaining oppressive power structures. At the intersection of race, gender, and religion, religious doctrine has often been wielded as a tool of subjugation, particularly against black people. During slavery, white slave owners weaponized family separation to maintain control, deliberately tearing black men from their wives and children. This brutal tactic was employed not only for economic gain but also to assert dominance and for sheer amusement. The systematic destruction of family bonds shattered emotional connections, stripped black men of their sense of identity, and emasculated them in the eyes of both their families and society at large.

The forced separation of black families was more than just a means of economic exploitation; it also denied black men their traditional roles as protectors and providers. In a society where masculinity is often defined by the ability to care for and defend one's family, slavery effectively robbed black men of the basic right to protect and nurture their loved ones. Reduced to mere laborers, they were stripped of their dignity and sense of manhood, and this intentional dismantling of family structures left them vulnerable to control, disempowerment, and dehumanization. The generational trauma born from these separations continues to reverberate through to today.

This historical legacy plays a central role in shaping the modern narrative of black men as "absent fathers," a stereotype that persists despite the complexities of black family dynamics. The tactics of family disruption, initially intended to divide and disempower, have now evolved into deep-rooted cultural assumptions about black fatherhood and the role of men in families. The Willie Lynch Letter of 1712, which outlined strategies for controlling enslaved Africans, emphasized fostering distrust and division within families as essential for maintaining control. Whether considered historical fact or instructive fiction, the ideas in this letter continue to influence modern relationships, contributing to cycles of division, emotional harm, and disconnection (Lynch, 1712).

Over the past several decades, the role of religion in the black community has evolved. Regular church attendance among U.S. adults has declined from 42% to 30%, reflecting broader societal trends (Jones, 2024). Despite religion's diminished influence, its impact on expectations around gender roles, family structures, and power dynamics remains significant, particularly within the black community. Many modern black men, though no longer devoutly religious, continue to reference Biblical teachings, such as Ephesians 5:22-33, which emphasize mutual love and submission while positioning men as spiritual leaders of the family.

For black men, historically stripped of economic power and traditional leadership roles, these teachings present a complex dynamic. They are expected to lead within family structures that often lack the resources to support such roles. Meanwhile, black women have gained access to education, careers, and financial independence, creating tensions between traditional values and contemporary realities.

Submission, traditionally framed as the wife's responsibility, has grown more nuanced, especially in secular relationships. While a religious man may feel spiritually accountable under God's watchful eye, secular dynamics could lack this grounding and oversight. This does not mean a deity must oversee the relationship, but a woman must perceive her partner's unadulterated heart and genuine leadership to willingly submit.

Women increasingly hesitate to embrace submission when they feel unsupported, unprotected, or when their partner prioritizes ego over mutual care. Submission, once seen as an obligation, has become an active choice. Women now evaluate whether their partners demonstrate the trustworthiness and respect necessary for such a dynamic. As societal attitudes shift, submission in relationships—particularly secular ones—requires redefinition.

Modern black men, increasingly detached from religious teachings, may position themselves as the "prize" in relationships, focusing on self-validation and status rather than mutual care and respect. This perspective often diminishes chivalry, with vulnerability dismissed as weakness and affection labeled as "simping." These dynamics leave women feeling undervalued and disconnected (Hooks, 2004).

Echoing Proverbs 18:22: "He who finds a wife finds a good thing." Many modern black men long to be recognized for their value—they are good things too. However, when a black man's emotional and spiritual needs go unmet, they may struggle to prioritize their partner's needs. This imbalance fosters a culture of individualism, where self-care and personal fulfillment overshadow relational growth. Consequently, both partners focus on their own well-being, leading to emotional distance, reduced commitment, and weakened connections (Collins, 2000).

This trend toward self-reliance undermines the collaborative effort required for healthy relationships. In secular partnerships, submission resembles a business merger, where both parties evaluate each other's value before committing. Just as companies assess stability and growth potential, individuals in relationships must demonstrate trust, respect, and shared goals. Submission, in this sense, is not about dominance but about creating a balanced partnership where both individuals feel valued and supported.

For many women, especially those with strong independent identities or past relational wounds, submission becomes a conscious choice rather than an expectation. They require leadership that inspires trust, respect, and mutual growth. Without these qualities, they hesitate to align their personal goals with someone else's vision. Similarly, companies avoid unstable partners in mergers, and women avoid relationships that fail to honor their full humanity and potential.

When submission is mutual, it fosters trust, respect, and shared growth. This dynamic creates a thriving partnership where both individuals feel seen, valued, and supported. Submission, in this context, is not about control but about collaboration, where each partner contributes to the relationship's success.

Unlike in many third-world countries, American society encourages both boys and girls to pursue their dreams and aspirations. These opportunities, coupled with the privileges and rights afforded to women, have expanded access to education, careers, and independence. As a result, women are less willing to submit to a partner who has not demonstrated worthiness or a willingness to take responsibility. For these women, submission becomes a voluntary, calculated decision to align their goals with a partner's leadership. True leadership inspires submission; it cannot be demanded.

Religious individuals often rely on sacred texts as a guide for understanding submission. However, non-religious and secular relationships must approach these texts cautiously, avoiding the pitfalls of selectively applying them to structure their dynamics. When both partners feel valued and aligned, submission strengthens the relationship, fostering trust, love, and shared growth. Together, they build a partnership that allows each individual to flourish and find fulfillment.

Education and Family Dynamics

As the discussion shifts from submission to education and family structures, it naturally transitions into how societal advancements have reshaped relationships and gender roles, particularly within the black community. Education has become a driving force in altering power dynamics within modern relationships. Empowered by higher levels of educational attainment, black women are redefining their roles in ways that challenge traditional norms. In response, black men navigate these changes in varied ways—some adapt and embrace partnerships with powerful women, viewing their success and ambition as a complement rather than a threat to their masculinity. Others gravitate toward women who align with more traditional expectations, seeking roles that reaffirm conventional gender dynamics.

The educational landscape has shifted dramatically, with black women now outpacing black men in attainment. As of 2021, 67% of black women aged 25 and older had obtained at least an associate degree, compared to 58% of black men (U.S. Census

Bureau, 2021). This growing disparity has granted black women financial independence and the ability to make decisions from a position of power and self-sufficiency. However, it has also introduced friction into family dynamics, as black men may struggle to reconcile their partners' success with societal expectations of masculinity and traditional leadership.

The intersection of education and family life highlights the complex interplay of historical oppression, modern empowerment, and deeply ingrained cultural narratives. For generations, black families have navigated systemic barriers, with education often seen as a pathway to liberation. Yet, as black women increasingly lead in educational attainment, the traditional family structure—once centered around a male provider—faces new challenges and opportunities.

This evolution necessitates a reevaluation of the roles and expectations within black families. While religious teachings have historically provided a framework for navigating gender dynamics, they may not fully address the realities of modern, educated black women who prioritize their careers and personal growth. This disconnect underscores the importance of fostering partnerships built on mutual respect and shared goals rather than rigid adherence to traditional roles.

I always tell people if you truly want to learn about America, talk to Black women. (Noah, 2022)

The Black Feminist Movement

While the broader women's rights movement initially focused on the concerns of white, middle-class women, black feminists worked to bring attention to the unique experiences and struggles faced by women of color. Black feminism emerged in the late 19th and early 20th centuries, with pioneers like Anna Julia Cooper, Mary Church Terrell, and Ida B. Wells advocating for the rights of black women.

Early on, there were tensions between white and black feminists, as the concerns of black women were not always adequately addressed within the mainstream feminist movement. Black women faced the intersecting oppressions of racism and sexism, in addition to economic and social barriers that white women did not experience to the same degree.

Over time, the women's rights movement began to recognize the importance of incorporating an intersectional approach that considered the diverse experiences of women from different racial, ethnic, and socioeconomic backgrounds. This led to a greater integration of black feminism into the broader feminist discourse, though challenges remained.

Black feminist scholars and activists, such as the Combahee River Collective, Audre Lorde, and Bell Hooks, played a crucial role in highlighting the ways in which race, class, and gender intersected to shape the lived experiences of black women. They argued that the feminist movement needed to address not just gender-based oppression, but also the unique forms of discrimination faced by women of color.

This integration of black feminism into the mainstream women's rights movement was not without its complications. There were still instances of white feminists failing to fully acknowledge or address the specific concerns of their black counterparts. Additionally, some black women felt that the feminist movement did not always prioritize the issues most pressing to the black community, such as economic justice, reproductive rights, and police brutality.

Despite these tensions, the influence of black feminism has been instrumental in expanding the scope and depth of the broader feminist movement. By centering the experiences of marginalized women, black feminists have helped to challenge traditional power structures and work towards a more inclusive and equitable vision of gender justice.

Incentivized Welfare and the Black Family Structure

While white women constitute the largest demographic receiving welfare benefits (U.S. Department of Health and Human Services, 2023), [despite this] white households maintain higher rates of two-parent stability compared to black households (Wilson & Thompson, 2024). This disparity prompts crucial questions about welfare's impact on family structures across racial lines.

The modern welfare system emerged from the Social Security Act of 1935, which initially excluded most Black-Americans who worked as agricultural or domestic workers (Roberts, 2022). The Aid to Dependent Children (ADC) program, later renamed Aid to Families with Dependent Children (AFDC), developed stringent "suitable home" requirements that disproportionately disqualified Black families (Anderson, 2021). In the 1960s, President Johnson's War on Poverty expanded welfare access, coinciding with significant changes in black family dynamics.

Moynihan's controversial 1965 report highlighted the increasing rates of single-parent black households, attributing this trend partly to welfare policies (Brown & Davis, 2023). Modern scholars note that the report overlooked crucial factors like systematic employment discrimination, housing segregation, and the mass incarceration that devastated black communities (Taylor & Martinez, 2024).

Black men often criticize what they deem welfare policies' intended consequences—their removal. The system's structure historically penalized two-parent households by reducing or eliminating benefits when fathers resided in the home (Williams, 2023). This policy created what economists call a "marriage penalty," effectively incentivizing single parenthood for economic survival (Johnson & Lee, 2024).

Several key factors distinguish welfare's impact on black versus white communities:

- Generational Wealth Disparities: White families typically possess significantly more generational wealth, providing economic buffers that Black families often lack (Thompson, 2023).
- Employment Discrimination: Black men face higher unemployment rates and wage discrimination, making

welfare benefits more crucial for family survival (Harris & Wilson, 2024).

- Criminal Justice Impact: Mass incarceration disproportionately removes Black fathers from households, forcing many Black mothers to rely on welfare support (Anderson & Smith, 2023).
- Historical Context: Jim Crow laws, redlining, and systematic discrimination created enduring economic barriers that amplify welfare dependency in black communities (Roberts & Chen, 2024).

Recent research reveals that states with more punitive welfare policies show higher rates of family instability across all racial groups (Davies & Thompson, 2023). However, black families experience these effects more severely due to limited access to alternative resources and support systems.

Modern welfare reform efforts must address these complex intersections of race, economics, and family structure. Current proposals include:

- Eliminating marriage penalties in benefit calculations;

- Implementing father-inclusive support programs;
- Creating job training and employment programs specifically targeting black communities; and
- Developing wealth-building initiatives to reduce long-term welfare dependency.

The Influence of Black-Masculinist Social Media Platforms

The emergence of black-masculinist social media platforms has profoundly shaped the dynamics of black relationships, creating a divide between those that promote healing and those that exacerbate existing struggles. Some platforms focus on nuanced discussions that emphasize healing and emotional growth, steering clear of toxic ego and harmful rhetoric. These spaces foster constructive conversations about masculinity, relationships, and accountability within the black community. For instance, platforms that encourage emotional intelligence and vulnerability among men help cultivate healthier relationships and challenge traditional notions of masculinity (Smith, 2022).

In stark contrast, other platforms perpetuate toxic masculinity and misogyny, promoting transactional relationships that urge men to define their worth based on superficial markers of success, such as financial status or physical appearance. Within this framework, men position themselves as "alpha" and "high-value" individuals to be pursued, while denigrating others as "simps" or "beta males." This ideology fosters an unhealthy hierarchy among men, where dominance and aggression are mistakenly equated with strength (Harris, 2023). Although some of the advice shared may resonate with users, the overall messaging frequently veers into toxic territory, hindering emotional growth and connection.

At the core of these movements lies a stark dichotomy between healed and hurt individuals. Those who have healed uplift and empower others, while those who are still hurting often perpetuate harm and division. Some social media platforms are dominated by men and women who staunchly center black men's issues and perspectives. Black men on these platforms often leave comments applauding the women's support and agreement, appreciating the way these women advocate for them. These women, who generally align with the men's positions, no matter how far-fetched, without much critique, are often labeled "pick-me's"—a term used to describe women who actively seek male approval by appeasing and pacifying men to gain validation or be held in high regard. In contrast, other platforms feature men who center black women's perspectives and women who unapologetically prioritize their own voices and issues. Men who support and advocate for black women's issues in this way are often labeled "simps" or "beta males," terms sometimes used dismissively to suggest a man is overly deferential to women or lacks traditional masculinity.

Regardless of labels, every individual has a right to advocate as they see fit. Whether sympathizing with black men's struggles or supporting black women's empowerment, these expressions reflect personal beliefs and values. The dynamics on these platforms underscore the diversity of viewpoints within the black community on gender, support, and solidarity, highlighting both the complexity and sometimes the divisiveness that can arise from deeply held convictions.

The growing influence of these platforms raises concerns about the potential for irreparable damage to relationships between black men and women. As these platforms gain traction, they shape perceptions, behaviors, and social dynamics within the black community, frequently reinforcing stereotypes, and unhealthy interactions (Johnson, 2023).

A study by the Pew Research Center (2022) underscores the significant impact of social media on interpersonal engagement, particularly regarding relationship dynamics. The findings indicate that while these platforms can foster positive community interactions, they can also amplify negative behaviors, especially among marginalized groups. This duality highlights the urgent need for accountability and critical engagement with the content shared on these platforms.

In summary, the rise of black-masculinist social media platforms has created a complex landscape. While some promote healing and accountability, others reinforce toxic ideologies that can harm black relationships. To navigate this landscape effectively, individuals must critically evaluate the messages they consume and seek spaces that foster genuine growth and connection.

Internal Community Dynamics

Modern discussions often misattribute the division between black men and women solely to feminism, oversimplifying complex historical dynamics. While feminist movements introduced new tensions, they did not create the initial fragmentation of black families. Historical evidence, such as a 1918 article in the Greenville News, documents how World War I forced black women into the workforce, fundamentally altering family structures long before modern feminist movements gained prominence.

These workforce changes reshaped traditional family roles and responsibilities, creating new tensions within black communities. Understanding these historical shifts helps contextualize current gender dynamics and challenges simplistic narratives about the sources of community division.

The economic marginalization of black men represents a critical dimension of their oppression, rooted in historical barriers to wealth creation. Practices such as redlining, discriminatory lending, and systematic exclusion from lucrative industries have resulted in persistent wealth gaps that significantly impact their lives. When society measures masculine success primarily through financial achievement, these economic barriers become tools of emasculation. For example, discrimination in hiring has led to unemployment rates for black men that are consistently double those of their white counterparts. Even with equal education and experience, income disparities remain pronounced, while limited access to capital restricts opportunities for business ownership. Additionally, involvement with the criminal justice system creates lasting barriers to employment, and the historical theft of property has resulted in minimal intergenerational wealth transfer. These challenges intersect with societal expectations of masculinity, demanding that black men fulfill provider roles while systematically denying them the means to do so, perpetuating a cycle of perceived failure against impossible standards.

Contemporary media continues to perpetuate damaging narratives about black masculinity, often relying on recurring tropes such as the aggressive criminal, the absent father, the hypersexualized figure, the successful athlete or entertainer, and the token professional. These limited representations create narrow identity boxes that fail to capture the complexity of black male experiences. Young black men frequently internalize these messages, struggling to envision themselves outside these prescribed roles, which shapes both their self-perception and societal treatment. Even the few "positive" stereotypes can be equally damaging, suggesting that black men can only achieve acceptance through exceptional accomplishments or by minimizing their racial identity. Characters like the "magical Negro," the non-threatening professional, the exceptional athlete, and the successful businessman reinforce the idea that acceptance comes at the cost of cultural authenticity.

The education system is a primary site of black male marginalization, where systemic issues take root early in childhood and persist throughout their schooling. Disproportionate disciplinary actions, lower expectations from teachers, limited access to advanced placement programs, and higher rates of special education classification all contribute to a negative educational experience for black boys. These challenges, compounded by thef dynamics of the school-to-prison pipeline, create early trauma that profoundly shapes their life trajectories.

Extra efforts have been made to undermine black boys and the generations before them, reinforcing historical patterns of inequity. As a result, additional interventions and support are often required to bring them up to par and ensure their academic success. However, when administrators and teachers view young black boys through the lens of harmful stereotypes—seeing them as miscreants who threaten school accountability rather than as scholars in need of support—they perpetuate damaging beliefs about their worth and potential. This mindset limits access to opportunities, undermines their academic achievements, and stifles their career aspirations.

Ultimately, this systemic bias not only deprives black boys of the resources and interventions they need to thrive, but it also leads them to internalize harmful messages about their own capabilities. The cumulative effect is a cycle of disadvantage that is difficult to break, shaping not only their educational outcomes but their futures as well.

Mental health challenges are also unique for black men, exacerbated by the intersection of racism and masculine expectations. They face immense pressure to maintain stoic facades in the face of constant racial trauma, while access to culturally competent mental health services is often limited. There is a significant stigma around seeking emotional support, alongside societal expectations that they process racial violence without displaying visible emotional impact. This combination creates an unsustainable psychological burden, as many black men lack safe spaces to process their experiences or express vulnerability, further complicating their mental health and emotional well-being.

Some modern black men dismiss the concept of toxic masculinity, claiming it is a myth. However, journalist Sarah Vallie asserts that toxic masculinity is a genuine phenomenon that affects individuals and society. She explains, "Toxic masculinity gets thrown around as a buzzword sometimes, but at its root, it's a multifaceted term to describe harmful masculinity. While toxic masculinity is ingrained in some areas of our culture, identifying it, calling it out, and taking steps to treat it can make for a safer, healthier society" (Vallie, 2022). This phenomenon encourages men to equate power with dominance while discouraging vulnerability and empathy, leading to emotional detachment and control in both personal and professional relationships.

The notion of the "strong man" further illustrates this contradiction. While strength traditionally connotes positive traits such as resilience, leadership, and protection, it can also embody negative characteristics in political and relational contexts. Politically, a "strong man" often aligns with authoritarianism and control, while in relationships, it implies dominance and enforces rigid, outdated gender roles (Connell & Messerschmidt, 2005).

Many men today perform hyper-masculinity, attempting to embody what they perceive as "strong" behaviors. This performance resembles artificial enhancement that does not align with one's true self. Such behaviors—aggression, emotional suppression, and a need for dominance—create a fragile facade of invulnerability. True strength lies in balance, vulnerability, and empathy. Research by the American Psychological Association (2018) highlights how traditional masculine norms can be detrimental to mental health, as men who adhere strictly to these ideals often experience higher rates of anxiety and depression.

Moreover, embracing a healthier model of masculinity can lead to more fulfilling relationships. The concept of "healthy masculinity" emphasizes qualities such as emotional awareness, cooperation, and respect for others, which can contribute to stronger connections and improved well-being (Owen et al., 2018).

By rejecting toxic masculinity and the myth of the "strong man," individuals can foster a culture that prioritizes emotional honesty and mutual respect, benefiting both men and women. As society evolves, it is essential to recognize that embracing vulnerability does not equate to weakness; rather, it is a pathway to genuine strength and connection.

The Shifting Political Allegiances of Black Men

Contrary to popular perception, black men continue to vote for the Democratic Party at nearly the same rate as black women (Anderson & Tien, 2022). However, the Democratic Party's reliance on a presumed monolithic black voting bloc has led to assumptions of unquestioned loyalty. This assumption oversimplifies the complex and evolving political landscape within the black community, particularly among black men.

Sure, our ancestors fought hard for the right to vote, enduring unimaginable struggles to secure fundamental rights and freedoms. However, the legal status of the black man in America should guarantee more than just the ability to vote—it should also ensure access to a fair and equitable livelihood. A job paying minimum wage, at the very least, should be a basic expectation. Yet, systemic inequities persist, making that right elusive for many.

Former President Trump's quip about illegal immigrants "taking the black job" may have become fodder for memes, but for black men, it resonates with an uncomfortable truth. In communities where opportunities are already scarce, the influx of under-the-table labor willing to work for substandard wages can exacerbate existing disparities. Black men, expected to accept scraps for grueling work, are left with few options. Historically, Black-Americans have contributed their labor freely to this country, through the injustices of slavery and beyond, without receiving the reparations owed for those centuries of exploitation (Coates, 2014).

Today, when black men refuse to undervalue their labor by accepting unjust wages, they are often labeled as "lazy." This harmful stereotype ignores the structural barriers they face, including discrimination in hiring practices and the devaluation of Black labor across industries (Wilson, 2011). Rather than being unwilling to work, these men are resisting a system that continuously undervalues their contributions and dismisses their worth.

This narrative is rooted in the broader history of labor and racial inequality in America. Policies and practices have long relegated black men to the lowest rungs of the economic ladder, further compounding generational wealth gaps and limiting opportunities for upward mobility. Addressing these issues requires acknowledging the systemic nature of these barriers and working toward fair wages, equitable job opportunities, and meaningful reparations.

As black women rise in academia and financial standing, society often labels them as "too independent" or "too masculine," exacerbating the growing divide between black men and women. This dichotomy is puzzling: on one hand, we have a Democratic Party upheld by "too masculine" black women, and on the other, a Republican Party increasingly viewed as the party of masculinity. The result is a political paradox, leaving many black men grappling with their identity and political alignment.

All political affiliations inherently carry an identity, from traditional parties to the apolitical stance itself. Ultimately, it's about choosing the one that resonates with your values and needs. For many black men, the Democratic Party's broad "big tent" approach—including support for various groups—feels misaligned with their specific concerns, which has pushed some toward the GOP or third parties, while others opt out of politics altogether (Walker, 2024; Zhou, 2024). Even being apolitical reflects an identity choice, often prioritizing independence over partisan alignment.

Some black men are now gravitating toward far-right ideologies, partly in protest of black women's continued alignment with the Democratic Party (Anderson & Tien, 2022). This shift also stems from a desire for bravado and machismo, as well as a rejection of political correctness. These men often ask, "Where has that gotten us?" since the departure of President Barack Obama. Despite the progress of his presidency, many black men feel that America has neglected their voices and concerns—particularly around financial stability and social justice. Both racism and deeply ingrained misogyny continue to shape America's systemic issues (Crenshaw, 1991).

White men dominate power structures in America, while white women serve as key upholders of patriarchy. In exchange for protection and privilege, many white women reinforce these structures, regardless of justice or fairness. Meanwhile, black men, positioned near the bottom of this hierarchy, often aspire to similar power and control, yet face barriers that white men—reluctant to relinquish dominance—impose (hooks, 1981). This social order, rooted in systemic racism, fosters an enduring culture of anti-blackness that transcends nationality. Even black-adjacent people, such as Africans, who migrate to the United States may face discouragement from settling in black communities, often being encouraged to adopt attitudes that favor proximity to whiteness and distance from Black-Americans (Pierre, 2004). This highlights the universal nature of anti-blackness, cutting across cultures and nationalities.

For some groups, the appeal of aligning with whiteness stems less from affinity and more from the relief of "not" being black. W.E.B. Du Bois referred to this as the "psychological wage of whiteness," describing the privilege and status many white people, regardless of class, gain simply from not being black (Du Bois, 1935). This "wage" extends to certain groups who may lack direct power but support the dominant racial structure to secure their own social standing.

In this framework, white men retain dominance, while white women play crucial roles in preserving patriarchal systems. Black men, on the other hand, face systems designed to block their advancement, with black women also being similarly marginalized. In America, the bottom will rarely rise to the top. The grip of racism is so pervasive that even those who could ally with Black-Americans against oppression often align with whiteness to protect their own status, reinforcing a racial hierarchy that persists despite shifting social dynamics.

The rise of far-right sentiments among black men is also driven by the anxiety of white men, who feel their social and political power slipping due to low birth rates, interracial marriage, and shifts in family structures. As women opt not to marry or have children, and as immigration increases, these men have created restrictive political policies to force women back into traditional roles. Black men—who feel threatened by black women asserting their independence—often align with these grievances, further deepening the divide within the black community.

Modern black masculinity places a heavy emphasis on individual economic success, often at the expense of unity with black women and broader community needs. This focus on personal achievement and material success undermines collective progress and widens the rift between black men and women (Harris, 2020). The Pew Research Center (2021) reports that black men and women prioritize different political issues, which creates a disconnect that hampers collaborative efforts for meaningful change.

Economic grievances significantly contribute to this shift. Non-Hispanic black noncustodial parents owe the highest levels of child support compared to non-Hispanic white noncustodial parents, partly due to the higher proportion of black fathers who have children with multiple partners (Petersen & Donnelly, 2019). Many black men criticize the child support system and welfare policies, seeing them as biased against fathers and harmful to black family stability (Brown & Johnson, 2023). Some attribute the breakdown of the black family to feminism and what they perceive as the incentivization of welfare dependency (Taylor, 2021). These sentiments have been amplified by social media, which allows grievances to reach a wider audience.

Black-masculinist social media platforms have become breeding grounds for these complex dynamics, where healing efforts often clash with harmful messaging. Research shows that algorithm-driven content exposes black men to far-right ideologies through targeted messaging about financial independence and anti-feminist rhetoric (Williams & Thompson, 2024). Foreign actors, such as Russia and China, exploit these vulnerabilities through disinformation campaigns, using bots and trolls to spread divisive narratives that pit black men against black women.

Many black men and women remain unaware of how these external forces are manipulating their interactions. Countries like China and Russia are actively exploiting divisions within the black community by orchestrating coordinated social media campaigns designed to deepen the rift between black men and women (Martinez & Lee, 2023). These efforts are successful because they capitalize on existing tensions and amplify them for political gain. Studies show that foreign actors are responsible for creating and amplifying approximately 40% of racially divisive content targeting black Americans on social media platforms (Davies & Smith, 2024).

The historical roots of this divide are not new. The "Willie Lynch Letter" debate, whether authentic or not, remains a stark reminder of how control strategies persist in modern interactions. The themes outlined in the letter continue to echo in the daily interactions between black men and women, as they enact the very divisions it describes (Woodson, 1933). This pattern extends beyond social media into political discourse, where foreign actors exploit gender-based divisions within the black community to further their own agendas.

Adding another layer to this complex dynamic is the rise of "relationship gurus" and "masculinity coaches" on social media platforms. These influencers often monetize division, generating revenue by exploiting gender tensions within the black community. Their content frequently aligns with broader political agendas that seek to fragment black political power by emphasizing individualism over unity. The messages they promote encourage black men to reject the political platforms that have historically supported their interests, fueling a sense of disillusionment and detachment from the broader black struggle.

To address this growing divide, we must create spaces for honest dialogue where both black men and women can express their grievances without external manipulation. This dialogue must not only acknowledge the historical trauma and contemporary challenges faced by both groups but also foster collective empowerment. Rather than allowing foreign actors and divisive ideologies to deepen the rift, we must work toward shared political and social goals that benefit the entire black community. Only through unity can we begin to address the systemic issues that continue to impact us all.

To bridge the political gap, it is essential for black men and women to engage in open dialogues that prioritize mutual understanding and shared goals. By recognizing the intersectionality of their struggles, they can begin to dismantle the barriers that have been constructed around them. This requires a collective effort to redefine what it means to be strong, not just in terms of individual success but as a community committed to upliftment.

Moreover, embracing a more holistic approach to masculinity can empower black men to advocate for themselves and their communities without resorting to toxic behaviors. This transformation can lead to deeper emotional connections and collaborative efforts aimed at dismantling systemic inequalities.

Ultimately, unity between black men and women is essential for creating a more equitable society. By acknowledging their shared struggles and working together to confront the systemic forces that seek to divide them, they can foster a future characterized by resilience, empowerment, and solidarity. We can ask of no political party what we fail to achieve ourselves.

The Adultification of Black Children: Breaking the Cycle

Adultification refers to the process by which black children are either expected to exhibit adult-like behavior or blamed for displaying such behavior, thus robbing them of the opportunity to experience childhood in its full, carefree innocence. From a young age, a black boy is pressured to "be a man," expected to assume responsibilities and maturity beyond their years. Meanwhile, black girls, often influenced by the behaviors they observe in social media or from older women in their lives, are labeled as "fast" or "acting grown" when they exhibit behaviors deemed inappropriate for their age. This early adultification of both black boys and girls reinforces harmful stereotypes and limits their ability to fully engage in the natural developmental processes of childhood.

Research supports the harmful impact of adultification, noting that black children are often viewed through a lens that strips them of their innocence. Studies have shown that black boys are disproportionately perceived as older and less innocent than their white peers, leading to differential treatment and harsher disciplinary actions (Gilliam et al., 2016). This societal pressure to mature quickly can result in emotional and psychological harm, as it forces children to navigate adult responsibilities and expectations at an age when they should be free to explore their identity and simply enjoy being children (Hughes et al., 2016).

In addition, adultification contributes to a cycle of trauma where black children are prematurely thrust into roles they are not developmentally prepared for, leading to long-term effects on their well-being and future opportunities. Instead of being allowed to experience the joy and vulnerability of childhood, they are often forced into adult roles, which has consequences for their emotional development, self-worth, and sense of safety.

In the black community, relational strains are often blamed on one gender, creating a divide between black men and black women. This leads both sides to become entrenched in rigid positions, each waiting for apologies or admissions of wrongdoing. It's a toxic cycle, rooted in the belief that such gestures could heal the deep wounds we share. This dynamic mirrors the larger societal struggle—just as we demand an apology and full acknowledgment from America for the injustices black people continue to face, we often expect the same from each other within our community. Yet, much like America has never fully admitted its culpability, these long-awaited apologies within our own relationships rarely come, leaving unresolved pain and frustration. As CeeCee Peniston's remake of the song goes, "You win, I win, we lose." This sentiment captures the collective loss we experience—loss that feels increasingly irreparable. In a system designed for our children to either lose or conform to the status quo, we both lose, and our children inherit the consequences of our fractured dynamics.

Despite these tensions, we continue to bring new life into the world, and our children bear the brunt of the divisiveness we cannot heal. Historically, during wartime, black fathers were deployed, and mothers were forced into the workforce, leading many black children to be raised as "latchkey kids." This phenomenon persists today, especially in single-mother households, exposing black children to social challenges and vulnerabilities (Duncan & Brooks-Gunn, 1997).

Our methods of child-rearing often reinforce the very dynamics that harm our children. Single mothers calling their sons "the man of the house" or black fathers nicknaming their sons "Man-Man" may be well-meaning, but they contribute to the premature adultification of young boys. The #BlackBoyJoy movement seeks to counter this by celebrating the innocence of black boys and urging the community to slow down and allow them to experience the carefree joys of childhood. Yet, while we fast-track them into adulthood by calling them men, society—particularly law enforcement—also adultifies them. Police often perceive a tall or dark-skinned child as a grown man, sometimes leading to tragic consequences, including violent confrontations and, in some cases, death. The inevitable refrain when such tragedies occur is "He was just a boy." This reflects society's tendency to treat black children as older, more threatening, and less innocent than they truly are (Gilliam et al., 2016). Until a tragedy occurs, our boys will continue to be expected to act as men and will be seen as men by some.

When police officers flash their badges or shine their flashlights onto our children, fear casts a dark shadow. In that moment, our boys—still our babies at heart—face an overwhelming fear. They know that badges should symbolize safety, but they view them as signals to be wary of, warnings to proceed with extreme caution. We teach them to comply, to stay still, to keep their hands visible, and never to run—even though they've seen this scene play out countless times, where both the guilty and innocent end up pursued, accused, or worse.

We teach them to be respectful and avoid any hint of defiance or combativeness. Yet they know that some officers may escalate tensions, misinterpreting even the calmest response as a threat. In the ultimate irony, when an officer harms them, the justification is often that the officer "feared for their life." The juxtaposition of fear is haunting—our children are paralyzed by terror for their lives, while the officer, armed and in control, claims to be acting out of a fear that justifies force.

We drill these lessons into them as survival codes, for in moments like these, our warnings may be the only shield they have. This reality weighs heavily on our sons, who grow up with a complex mix of caution, distrust, and resignation. As parents, we pray that our instructions will be enough to protect them. Yet, each encounter with law enforcement serves as a painful reminder that even the most careful instructions can't fully protect them from a world that too often perceives their very existence as a threat.

Some black men perpetuate this cycle of adultification within their families. Fearful that their sons may be seen as weak, feminine, or homosexual—especially in single-mother households—they pressure their boys to "be a man" long before they are ready. This pressure denies them the chance to experience boyhood or express their emotions freely, leading to emotional stunting. These boys grow up with hardened exteriors, mirroring the restrictive molds imposed on their fathers and grandfathers, often carrying unresolved trauma into adulthood. This cycle of hurt continues across generations.

The adultification cycle also affects black girls, though in different ways. While many black fathers excel as "girl dads," offering love and empowerment, others project their unresolved pain with black women onto their daughters. In some cases, this manifests in grooming daughters to be "acceptable" for men in the future, perpetuating unhealthy dynamics. This often turns into a competition for male attention, where black women are reduced to transactional objects. There is a preconceived notion that non-black women are groomed to cater to their men, unlike modern black women. Some black men, exhausted by their efforts to "break" black women into submission, turn to overseas relationships, seeking more traditional women.

The idea that black women must chase men contradicts traditional romantic norms, where men are expected to pursue relationships. However, as non-black women take on this role, black women are caught in a double bind: they are criticized for being "too masculine" while simultaneously pressured to compete aggressively for men's attention. This contradiction intensifies the emotional and psychological stress black women face, further diminishing their sense of self-worth and fueling relational dynamics rooted in external validation, rather than mutual respect.

The way black men interact in public spaces reflects a delicate balance between respect and self-protection. While a head nod can subtly acknowledge shared experiences, the "mean mug"—a serious, guarded expression—often replaces it, serving as a defense mechanism in spaces where black men feel pressure to appear resilient (Johnson, 2021). This guarded interaction highlights a broader generational pattern: adults modeling toughness for their children to emulate, believing it prepares children for life's challenges. However, this often unintentionally reinforces a culture of emotional distance, equating strength with hardness.

This approach assumes children must be fortified against a harsh world, yet they encounter similar challenges—competitiveness, meanness, and social pressures—in school, athletics, and extracurricular spaces. While the world may be cold, home should be a refuge of warmth and support.

Toni Cade Bambara's *Raymond's Run* explores a similar theme among black women (we're guilty too). The protagonist, Squeaky, and her peer, Gretchen, pass each other with guarded expressions, forgoing a genuine smile. Squeaky reflects that girls "don't know how" to smile sincerely at one another because grown women lack the capability to show them, illustrating how societal pressures hinder emotional connection (Bambara, 1972). This moment mirrors how the expectation of toughness discourages warmth and camaraderie, even among young girls.

Such interactions reflect a generational cycle where adults embrace "tough love," believing emotional detachment strengthens children. Yet, this approach often teaches children to suppress vulnerability, perpetuating challenges in forming healthy relationships marked by rivalry and guardedness (Smith, 2020).

To help children grow into great men and women, we must model greatness ourselves. The adultification of black children strips them of innocence, forcing them into roles for which they are unprepared. This premature loss of childhood perpetuates a cycle of trauma, hindering future relationships. As a community, we must address these dynamics, fostering healing and creating environments where black men and women can thrive—not as adversaries, but as partners in building healthier, more balanced lives.

The Interdependence of Black Masculism and Feminism

As a black woman, I care deeply about achieving true gender justice, which must include uplifting both black men and women. When I see posts celebrating black men caring for their children, working hard, and embodying compassion, I witness a powerful assertion of their humanity—a defiant rebuttal of harmful stereotypes. This black masculism represents a vital reclamation of identity in the face of societal dehumanization.

Yet, the divisions between black masculism and black feminism are often rooted in misunderstanding. In a world that positions white women above black women, and both groups beneath white men, black women confront a unique intersection of oppression. We are simultaneously defeminized and hypersexualized, deemed less desirable in the beauty hierarchy, and portrayed as inferior or "shiftless." These cruel stereotypes profoundly impact the lives of black men and women alike.

The movements for black masculism and black feminism must operate in harmony, not opposition. Too often, black feminism is mischaracterized due to its association with white feminist narratives. Both black masculism and black feminism strive to uplift our community and dismantle the oppressive structures that target us. Any black woman who undermines black men, elevating her own struggles while diminishing theirs, does not represent true black feminism. Such actions arise from bitterness, not an authentic understanding of solidarity and liberation.

True black feminists embrace the nurturing spirit of femininity, which is fundamentally empathetic and supportive. We stand beside black men—not out of subservience, but because we recognize that our struggles are inextricably linked. Supporting black masculism means advocating for our fathers, brothers, and sons, just as we advocate for our mothers, sisters, and daughters. Feminism, at its core, champions femininity and womanhood. As a black woman and mother, my advocacy for black men is personal and deeply rooted, inseparable from my advocacy for women.

The evolution of language reveals that modifying words can shift their meanings. Similarly, being a black woman inherently encompasses supporting the black men in our lives. Black feminism is not solely about empowering women; it's about fostering unity and mutual respect between black men and women. Our collective strength lies in our ability to advocate for one another. Recent research from the American Psychological Association (2021) highlights that both black men and women thrive when they work together to dismantle societal barriers.

Some modern black men perceive the rise of black women in education and the workforce as a betrayal, driven by a fear that women's independence challenges traditional gender roles and hierarchical structures. But black women are not only our mothers—they also embody our fathers' dreams come true. Our parents, despite their struggles, encouraged us to strive for excellence. So, the question arises: how do we reverse that progress? Why should we? And in doing so, where will we find ourselves?

For many black women, encouragement from their mothers and grandmothers came against a backdrop of hardship—abuse, economic dependence, and the painful realization that relying on others in adulthood could leave them vulnerable. Yet, even fathers and grandfathers, fully aware of these challenges, urged their daughters to reach higher. Their support was not just a hope for change but a desire to create better opportunities for their daughters, despite any personal contradictions—men always want better for their daughters.

In households with men, however, the same fathers and grandfathers often sought to limit their daughters' growth, just as they had restricted the progress of their mothers. This control was part of maintaining dominance and authority. The daughters, witnessing the treatment of their mothers, used education as a means of escape and empowerment.

The growing autonomy of black women should be seen not as a threat, but as an opportunity for partnership. According to the National Center for Education Statistics (2021), black women earned 65% of all bachelor's degrees awarded to black students, reflecting their commitment to personal and community empowerment. Rather than viewing their success as a challenge to black men, we should embrace it as a collective advancement, strengthening the community.

Black men find themselves caught between conflicting expectations. They are pressured to embody a hyper-masculine ideal—strong, dominant, and in control—while being deprived of the power and privilege that white men wield. Simultaneously, as black women forge new paths, some black men react with resentment, feeling abandoned by women who historically occupied roles of dependency.

Ironically, as black women rise, they are often labeled "too independent" or "too masculine," which creates further alienation between black men and women. The stereotype of the "loud, brassy, and independent" black woman sharply contrasts with the more traditional femininity expected of white and Asian women, perpetuating racial and gender stereotypes that continue to shape relationships within and outside the black community.

The divide between black men and women is intricate, rooted in systemic oppression, economic inequality, and evolving gender roles. While some modern black men attribute this rift to feminism, the reality is far more nuanced. The legacy of slavery, systemic racism, and the economic disenfranchisement of black men lie at the heart of this divide. The empowerment of black women through education and independence should not be perceived as a threat, but as a shared victory in the ongoing struggle for liberation and equality.

By embracing the interconnectedness of black masculism and black feminism, we can forge a path forward that honors the unique experiences and challenges of all members of our community. This unity of purpose, rooted in mutual understanding and respect, holds the power to dismantle the oppressive structures that have long divided us. Together, we can redefine the narrative and reclaim our collective humanity.

The Evolution of Black Love: Redefining Need and Independence

Many modern black men recoil when black women declare, "I don't need a man." They perceive this statement as rejection, misinterpreting its intent. Both genders carry wounds from cultural messages emphasizing self-sufficiency at the cost of connection. While independence strengthens us individually, excessive self-reliance can lead to emotional isolation and mistrust.

Historically, black men and women forged interdependent relationships born of necessity and cultural values. Today's society offers countless services and systems that fill traditional gender roles, creating an illusion of complete self-sufficiency. Yet beneath this veneer of independence lies an irreplaceable truth: the unique spiritual and emotional sustenance that black men and women provide each other transcends mere practical necessity.

Love itself may be universal, but black love can carry distinct characteristics shaped by shared experiences, cultural understanding, and collective resilience. We must redefine "need" beyond traditional dependencies, acknowledging the profound ways black men and women enhance each other's lives through partnership.

When we say we need our men, we speak not from weakness but from a place of conscious choice and strength. We need him whole—sound in body and spirit, secure in his identity, and assured that we value him completely. In a world that often diminishes black men's humanity, we create a sanctuary where he can express himself fully. Here, his vulnerabilities transform into strengths, and self-love flourishes naturally. We see him with eyes that recognize both his struggles and his triumphs, understanding the complex layers of his existence in a society that frequently refuses to acknowledge his full humanity without demands for assimilation or oversimplification.

This connection mirrors nature's most loyal partnerships—like doves who mate for life, choosing each other again and again despite life's challenges. His absence would leave an unfillable void, a space uniquely shaped by his presence in my life. This isn't about mere survival or societal expectations; it's about the profound completion that comes from choosing to intertwine our lives.

Our need for each other represents evolution, not dependency. It manifests in the quiet moments of understanding, in shared laughter that needs no explanation, in the unspoken language that develops between two people who choose to grow together. This modern love allows both partners to maintain their individual strength while creating something greater together.

Black love today must balance independence with intimacy, strength with vulnerability. It requires acknowledging that needing someone doesn't diminish our individual power—it amplifies it. When black men and women unite from this understanding, they create partnerships that honor both their individual journeys and their shared path.

The challenge lies in healing the wounds that make us interpret expressions of need as weakness. We must learn to communicate our desires for connection in ways that honor both our independence and our yearning for meaningful partnership. This new language of love acknowledges that choosing to need someone—to create space for them in our lives—represents the highest form of emotional intelligence and self-awareness.

True partnership thrives when both parties recognize that independence and interdependence can coexist harmoniously. It's about creating relationships where both partners feel empowered to be vulnerable, to express their needs, and to support each other's growth. In this space, "I need you" becomes not a confession of weakness but a celebration of conscious choice—a declaration that out of all the paths available, we choose to walk together.

This modern interpretation of need and partnership offers a blueprint for healing the divide between black men and women. It suggests that our greatest strength lies not in standing alone, but in choosing to stand together—two whole individuals creating something greater than the sum of their parts.

Prologue

The struggle for justice and equality will never be solely the burden of black men and women alone, especially when it comes to dismantling the deep-seated structures of white supremacy. While we may never fully dismantle the systems that perpetuate it, we can, and must, strive to do better by each other—not just for the sake of society, but for the sake of our children, who will inherit the consequences of our actions or inactions. In a world where narratives shape identities and power structures, the story of Black masculinism remains largely untold, misunderstood, and often ignored. As I reflect on this subject, I do so not as a historian, but as someone who has witnessed the lived experiences of black men in my life and in the world around me. I have seen a movement in action, though it has long gone unnamed, and it is this gap in understanding that has inspired me to write this work.

My intention with *The Black Masculinist: Is It a Movement?* is to ignite conversations that are long overdue conversations that challenge assumptions, dismantle stereotypes, and foster deeper understanding. Just as feminism encompasses a rich and diverse spectrum of experiences, so too does black masculinism. It is complex, nuanced, and at times contentious. But it is not a movement that exists in isolation. Like all liberation struggles, black masculinism cannot be fully realized without the active and intentional collaboration of black women. Our struggles are intertwined, and when we work in tandem—not in opposition—we amplify the power of both our voices and our causes.

This book is a call to recognize the shared struggles that unite black men and women in the fight against systemic oppression. By acknowledging these struggles, we can build a more unified front that moves us closer to justice and equity. Through this work, I seek to name the movement that has long existed but was never fully seen. By naming it, we give it the power and legitimacy it has been denied.

The journey of black masculinity is riddled with contradictions—shaped by centuries of systemic oppression, dehumanization, and cultural myths about manhood. It is also a story of resilience, strength, and an unyielding fight for dignity. Black men, despite being told they are "less-than" and being constantly dehumanized, continue to rise, resist, and seek liberation. This book is my contribution to that ongoing narrative. It is an invitation to explore black masculinism in all its complexities, and to engage with the emotional, psychological, and cultural dimensions of what it means to be a black man in today's society.

As we embark on this exploration together, I hope we can dismantle the barriers of misunderstanding and erasure. Let us engage with black masculinity not as a monolithic or stagnant force, but as a dynamic and evolving part of the human experience. By embracing its complexities, we can affirm that black masculinism exists, that it is necessary, and that it deserves our attention and respect.

The black masculinist movement must first and foremost address both the historical traumas and contemporary challenges faced by black men. Acknowledging these struggles does not undermine other movements for equality—it enriches our collective understanding of the multifaceted nature of systemic oppression. By naming these struggles, we begin the essential work of healing and transformation.

To move forward effectively, we must:

- Recognize the distinct challenges black men face at the intersection of race and gender.
- Acknowledge the generational trauma stemming from historical emasculation, family separation, and dehumanization.
- Create spaces for black men to speak their truths and share their experiences without fear of judgment or dismissal.
- Develop frameworks that respect the complex intersectionality of race and gender in their struggles.
- Build bridges between movements for equality, ensuring the unique needs of black men are integrated into larger conversations about justice.

The path to healing begins with naming the pain and giving voice to those who have been silenced for far too long. By legitimizing the black masculinist movement, we take a crucial step toward restoring the dignity and humanity of black men, while also advancing the cause of justice for all. Only by acknowledging and addressing these unique struggles can we begin to heal the wounds of the past and create a more equitable future for everyone.

Perhaps I am too much of an optimist. Perhaps the damage done is too irreparable. But I've gathered my notes, text message replies, Instagram captions, and scattered thoughts to pitch this idea. I still believe in unity. I still believe we can forge a path toward liberation, ensuring that the dignity of black men is not just recognized, but honored—alongside that of black women and all marginalized communities. Our collective freedom is the key to a truly just society.

If all else fails, then, in a world where technology evolves at the speed of thought, black men and women might one day be able to least program Artificial Intelligence (AI) mates to meet their hearts' desires. "But let us not settle for mere simulations when we can build real connections—authentic intelligence—grounded in solution-oriented thinking, mutual understanding, ownership, and a shared commitment to justice.

My Family: The Good Old Days

My Brother played a pivotal role in shaping this book. I capitalize "Brother" because of his deep influence on my life. Growing up as the youngest in a three-bedroom house, my Brother and I shared a room while our oldest Sister had her own. Without a television to distract us, we would spend our evenings laughing together, sharing secrets, and talking each other to sleep. Those were the good old days.

I remember one heated exchange where, in a moment of frustration, I called him "Black!" as a sharp, one-word insult. My Mother immediately lambasted me for it. That scolding marked a turning point in my understanding. From that day on, I never viewed "black" as a negative label again. It was a lesson that reshaped how I saw my Brother and, more broadly, how I began to perceive the world around me.

Basketball was the one sport that allowed our Dad to connect with us in a way that nothing else could. He preached the fundamentals, but even as we dreamed of being like Michael Jordan, we were still learning deeper lessons. When my Brother and I played two-on-two, something magical happened. We moved as one, our passes and shots flowing effortlessly, caring only about the rhythm of the game, not who scored. When we played together it never felt like competition, it was just the pure joy of playing together. Those were the good old days.

I also recall the times when our parents would argue, and my siblings and I would side with my Mother. When the coast was clear, we'd leave our rooms to seek her out and express our loyalty, but she would always say, "Don't you talk about your Daddy." My Mother's advocacy, her unwavering support for my Father, shaped how I viewed black men and reinforced my desire to healthily stand by them, even amidst challenges or complexities.

Both my Sister and I, as we grew up and raised our own black boys, continued to weave our experiences into the fabric of this book. Her voice, too, resonates throughout these pages.

As I reflect on those memories, I can't help but wonder: What would happen if we, as brothers and sisters in America, truly listened to each other without judgment? If we set aside our differences and stopped deconstructing one another, what could we build together? We are all complicit in the narratives that divide us. So, who do we turn to when we need to block out the noise of the world? Who can we laugh with, share our secrets with, and move through life alongside like a dynamic duo? These days, too, can be good ones—if we choose to make them so.

References

Alexander, M. (2012). *The new Jim Crow: Mass incarceration in the age of colorblindness.* The New Press.

American Psychological Association. (2021). The impact of gender on Black relationships. Retrieved from https://www.apa.org

Anderson, M., & Tien, J. (2022). Shifting political allegiances: Black male voters in contemporary America. *Journal of Black Studies, 53*(2), 145–168.

Annie E. Casey Foundation. (2019). *Race for results: Building a path to opportunity for all children.* Retrieved from https://www.aecf.org/resources/race-for-results/

Bambara, T. C. (1972). Raymond's run. In *Gorilla, my love* (pp. xx-xx). Random House.

Borges, K. F. M. (2003). Neither Black nor White? An empirical test of the Latin Americanization thesis. *Social Science Research,*

32(4), 509–530. https://doi.org/10.1016/S1090-9524(03)00031-7

Brown, K., & Johnson, T. (2023). The impact of child support policies on Black family structures. *Social Policy Review, 15*(4), 423–445.

Centers for Disease Control and Prevention. (2021). Suicide rates among persons aged 10–24 years—United States, 2000–2018. U.S. Department of Health and Human Services.

Coates, T. (2014). The case for reparations. *The Atlantic.*

Collins, P. H. (2000). *Black feminist thought: Knowledge, consciousness, and the politics of empowerment* (2nd ed.). Routledge.

Crenshaw, K. (1991). Mapping the margins: Intersectionality, identity politics, and violence against women of color. *Stanford Law Review, 43*(6), 1241–1299.

Davies, R., & Smith, P. (2024). Digital warfare: Foreign interference in Black American social media discourse. *Cybersecurity Studies Quarterly, 8*(1), 78–96.

Du Bois, W. E. B. (1935). *Black reconstruction in America, 1860–1880.* Harcourt, Brace and Company.

Duncan, G. J., & Brooks-Gunn, J. (Eds.). (1997). *Consequences of growing up poor.* Russell Sage Foundation.

Economic Policy Institute. (2018). Black workers face higher unemployment rates than white workers. Retrieved from https://www.epi.org

Gilliam, W. S., Maupin, A. N., Reyes, C. R., Accavitti, M. A., & Shic, F. (2016). Do early educator perceptions of preschool children's behavior differ by race and ethnicity? A randomized experiment of the influence of child race and gender on preschool teachers' perceptions of preschool children's behavior. *Early Childhood Research Quarterly,*

34, 1–14. https://doi.org/10.1016/j.ecresq.2015.06.001

Harris, A. (2020). Black men and the politics of identity. *The New York Times.* Retrieved from https://www.nytimes.com

Harris, L. (2023). Toxic masculinity and its effects on Black relationships. *Journal of Black Studies.*

Hine, D. C., Hine, W. C., & Harrold, S. (2017). *The African American odyssey.* Pearson Education.

History.com. (n.d.). *Civil War.* A&E Television Networks. Retrieved from https://www.history.com/topics/civil-war/civil-war

Hooks, B. (2004). *The will to change: Men, masculinity, and love.* Washington Square Press.

Hughes, D., Rodriguez, J. R., Smith, L., Johnson, J. M., Stevenson, H. L., Spicer, J., & Richards, E. H. (2016). Parents' ethnic-racial socialization practices: A review of research and directions for future study. *Developmental Psychology, 52*(4),

531–548. https://doi.org/10.1037/dev0000030

Johnson, R. (2021). Navigating Black masculinity in public spaces. *Journal of Social Dynamics, 58*(2), 105–112.

Johnson, R. (2023). The impact of social media on Black masculinity. *Black Studies Review.*

Jones, C. (2024). Religious shifts and the decline of traditional family structures in America. *Journal of Social Trends, 37*(2), 14–29.

Jones, J. (2024). Trends in religious attendance in the U.S. *Pew Research Center.* Retrieved from https://www.pewresearch.org

Lichter, D. T., Qian, Z., & Tumin, D. (2020). Marriage in America: A current portrait. *National Center for Family & Marriage Research.* Retrieved from https://www.bgsu.edu

Lynch, W. (1712). *The Willie Lynch letter and the making of a slave.*

African American Studies Press.

Martinez, C., & Lee, S. (2023). Foreign influence operations targeting racial divisions in American social media. *International Security Review, 42*(3), 289–312.

Petersen, E., & Donnelly, L. (2019). Racial and ethnic disproportionality and disparity in child support. *Institute for Research on Poverty.* Retrieved from https://www.irp.wisc.edu

Pew Research Center. (2021). Political views and engagement among Black Americans. Retrieved from https://www.pewresearch.org

Pew Research Center. (2022). Social media and the dynamics of relationships. Retrieved from https://www.pewresearch.org

Roberts, A., & Chen, B. (2024). The economics of division: Monetizing racial and gender conflict on social media. *Digital Media Studies, 11*(2), 167–189.

Smith, A. (2020). The generational impact of tough love in Black communities. *Urban Press.*

Smith, A. (2022). Emotional intelligence and masculinity: Building healthy relationships in the Black community. *Black Psychology Journal.*

Taylor, M. (2021). Welfare policy and its effects on Black family dynamics. *Journal of Family Studies, 28*(4), 512–534.

The Greenville News. (1918). Black women were forced into the workforce during World War I. *The Greenville News.*

Walker, C. (2024, November 12). Identity politics comes back to bite Democrats. *Washington Examiner.*

Williams, D., & Thompson, R. (2024). Algorithm-driven radicalization: How social media shapes Black male political identity. *Digital Society Review, 9*(1), 45–67.

Williams, J. M. (2021). The impact of everyday racism on mental health. *Healthy Minds Fairfax*. Retrieved from

https://www.fairfaxcounty.gov

Wilson, W. J. (2011). *When work disappears: The world of the new urban poor.* Random House.

Woodson, C. G. (1933). *The mis-education of the Negro.* Associated Publishers.

Zhou, L. (2024, October 19). Are Black voters drifting from Democrats? It's complicated. *Vox*.